Six Christmas Plays

SIX CHRISTMAS PLAYS

by

NOELENE MARTIN
and
JENNIE AUSTERBERRY

NATIONAL CHRISTIAN EDUCATION COUNCIL
Robert Denholm House
Nutfield, Redhill, Surrey, RH1 4HW

The plays in this book may be performed without written permission from the publishers provided that no admission charge is made for the performance. Where an admission charge is to be made for the performance, written application for performing rights must be made to the National Christian Education Council.

Cover design by Juliet Larder

British Library Cataloguing — in — Publication Data

Martin, Noelene
  Six Christmas Plays
  I. Title   II. Austerberry, Jennie
  822'.914   PR6063.A715/

ISBN 0-7197-0519-3

ISBN 0-7197-0519-3
Typeset by Avonset, Midsomer Norton, Bath
Printed and bound by Page Bros (Norwich) Ltd

CONTENTS

INTRODUCTION

The six short plays in this book are all suitable for performance near Christmas. The language is simple enough for them to be performed by children, but they will be most effective, both in the preparation and the presentation, if they are performed by mixed groups of adults and children. It is valuable for children to work together with older people, and better for them to portray characters of their own age than try to play adult parts. It is hoped that these plays will be used by church groups, school groups including staff, and family groups.

Three of the plays, *The Dream, A Little House*, and *'Let me in!'* are set in Bethlehem at the time of the nativity. Each has a new and intriguing slant on the traditional story.

No Room uses a time-switch to reinforce the truth that Christmas is not bound by time or place, but is as real and relevant today as it was 2000 years ago.

The Worst Christmas Play Ever is a short, modern fun-play which will appeal especially to children, and might be used as a 'filler' with other items, or as part of a carol concert.

A New Song is an imaginative reconstruction of the known events leading to the writing, singing, and subsequent popularisation of the carol *Silent Night, Holy Night!*.

THE DREAM

by

Noelene Martin

THE DREAM

CAST

JACOB, an innkeeper
SHEM, an innkeeper
Two STRANGERS
ELIZABETH, Jacob's wife
RUTH, Shem's daughter
A FATHER and his FAMILY
MARY
JOSEPH

The scene is a street in Bethlehem on the first Christmas Eve. Inns are placed Stage R and Stage L; one has the name JACOB'S INN over its door, the other SHEM'S INN.

SCENE 1

The two innkeepers, JACOB and SHEM, stand talking halfway between the doors of their inns.

Jacob   I've never seen Bethlehem so busy.

Shem   No, neither have I. They're all here because of this census.

Jacob   I've been run off my feet for the last few days. They ache all the time.

Shem   Mine too. Have you any empty rooms left?

Jacob   Only two, and they'll be filled by tonight, I'm sure.

Shem   I've only one left. From what I've heard, everywhere in the town is just about full.

> *Two STRANGERS enter, apparently in deep conversation. They continue to speak as they walk slowly across the stage in front of JACOB and SHEM.*

Stranger 1   Now let me repeat what you've just said. You say you were told in a dream that a king will come to Bethlehem tonight?

Stranger 2   *(nodding)* That's right. That was my dream.

Stranger 1   But which king, and why come to Bethlehem?

Stranger 2 I told you, I don't know. But the message was clear — tonight a king will be here in Bethlehem.

Stranger 1 *(shaking head)* I know you saw in a dream the coming of the rain which broke the drought last year, so I should believe you . . .

Stranger 2 But you don't. Well, we'll wait and see.

> *The two STRANGERS continue to walk off stage. The INNKEEPERS, who have listened to the conversation, watch them leave. Then they look at each other.*

Jacob Did you hear that? A king is coming to Bethlehem tonight.

Shem It was only that stranger's dream. You don't believe that, do you? *(He shakes his head)* Why would a king come to Bethlehem?

Jacob Perhaps he's travelling somewhere for this census too.

Shem *(slowly)* Possibly. I wonder where he'd stay? There is no palace here.

Jacob He might have to stay at an inn.

> *Their faces light up as the same thought occurs to them both.*

Shem Wouldn't it be wonderful if he stayed at *my* inn!

13

Jacob   *(excitedly)* Or mine! I must make sure there is a room left empty, just in case he calls.

Shem   Yes, I'm going to do the same. How exciting! *(He rushes inside his inn, calling to his daughter)* Ruth! Ruth!

              JACOB goes to the door of his inn where he meets his wife ELIZABETH.

Jacob   How many rooms are still empty, Elizabeth?

Elizabeth Some people have just gone into the back room, so that leaves only the top one to be filled.

Jacob   *(grasping her shoulders with his hands)* Good. I want it cleaned and made ready.

Elizabeth It is clean already. Is there someone important who wants the room?

Jacob   Someone important, yes, but I'm not sure yet if he wants it.

Elizabeth *(taking his hands from her shoulders)* What do you mean?

Jacob   I've heard that a king is coming to Bethlehem tonight and he might stay at our inn. I want that room spotless in case he comes here.

Elizabeth A king come here? You're joking! *(She*

14

laughs) If you want to give that room special attention you're going to have to do it yourself. I'm too busy with all the other people who want meals.

Jacob   *(folding his arms across his chest)*   All right, I will.

> *Unseen by the two engrossed in their argument, a FATHER and his FAMILY have entered, looking hopefully at the inn door. JACOB turns and sees them standing there.*

Father   Excuse me, sir, but do you have a room for my family for the night?

Jacob   *(unfolding his arms; speaking angrily)*   No, I'm sorry, we're full.

Father   We've tried everywhere else but they're all full. Are you sure you can't fit us in anywhere?

Jacob   No, I'm sorry.

Elizabeth   *(tugging at Jacob's sleeve)*   But what about the . . .

Jacob   *(brushing her off but still watching the man)*   As I said, I'm sorry but we're full. *(He points to Shem's Inn)* Have you tried that inn? I think they have a room.

Father   *(nodding his head tiredly)*   Thank you. Goodbye.

The FAMILY moves wearily towards the other inn. JACOB and ELIZABETH watch them.

Elizabeth   Why did you send that man away? His family looked so tired and we *do* have a room.

Jacob   I know, but don't you realise — if everywhere else is full then the king *must* stay here. Now I must prepare that room.

JACOB hurries away into his inn. ELIZABETH throws her hands up in the air, mutters something about a king, and follows him. The FATHER knocks at SHEM's door. SHEM answers it.

Father   *(wearily)*   Do you have any room for us in your inn, sir?

Shem   *(looking at the family)*   Room? For your family?

Father   Yes. We've walked all day and my children are tired and hungry.

Shem   *(slowly)*   Yes, I do have one room left. I was going to keep it for someone else, but you obviously need it. Come in and go straight up the stairs.

The FAMILY enters the inn. SHEM stands outside his door and is joined by his daughter RUTH.

Ruth   I thought you were going to keep that room for the king, Dad.

Shem   I was, Ruth, but I've changed my mind. If the king does come here, which is very unlikely, he will have to go somewhere else. Those poor people need shelter more than a rich king does.

> *SHEM hangs a 'Full' sign on his door and goes into the inn with RUTH. MARY and JOSEPH enter from the opposite side and MARY points to Jacob's Inn.*

Mary   Here is an inn, Joseph, and there is no sign outside. Perhaps we will be lucky this time.

> *JOSEPH knocks at the door and JACOB answers it. His expectant smiling face changes when he sees it is not the rich king he had hoped it would be.*

Joseph   Excuse me, sir, we were wondering . . .

Jacob   *(interrupting him)*   No, I'm sorry. We're full.

Joseph   But, sir, my wife is going to have a baby. We must have somewhere to stay the night.

Jacob   *(glancing at Mary but shaking his head)*   I understand, but really I can't help. I have no room. Perhaps you could try over there. *(He points to Shem's Inn)*

17

Joseph   *(very disappointed)*   Thank you.

> *JOSEPH and MARY walk very slowly towards the other inn. ELIZABETH joins JACOB outside their inn. Together they watch the weary pair.*

Elizabeth   Really, Jacob, you should have let those poor people have the room. What is that poor woman going to do?

Jacob   *(turning to face her)*   I don't know and I don't really care. That room is for a king, not a peasant baby.

> *JACOB and ELIZABETH go into their inn. JOSEPH knocks at Shem's door. SHEM opens it, glancing up to see if the 'Full' sign is still there.*

Joseph   Sir, do you have any room in your inn?

Shem   *(pointing to the sign)*   No, I'm sorry. I've just filled my last room.

Joseph   Haven't you anywhere we can stay? My wife is going to have a baby.

Shem   A baby. Oh dear. *(He points to Jacob's Inn)* Have you tried there?

Joseph   Yes, but his inn is full, too.

Shem   Hmm. *(He scratches his head)* There is no room inside but if you're really desperate you can stay in the stable with the animals. It isn't much, but it's all I can offer.

Joseph *(looking at Mary who nods)* Thank you, sir. We'll take it.

> *SHEM, MARY and JOSEPH leave the stage together.*

SCENE 2

The following morning. The two INNKEEPERS are again standing outside their inns, talking.

Shem You look rather weary this morning, Jacob. Didn't you get much sleep last night?

Jacob *(yawning)* No. I sat up half the night waiting for that king to knock on my door, but he didn't. A dream — ha! And I believed it! *(He looks closely at SHEM)* What about you? You look tired too. Did you also sit up waiting?

Shem Me? Oh, no. Our rooms were full anyway. No. A woman had a baby here last night and caused some excitement.

Jacob *(curiously)* Excitement? What kind of excitement?

Shem Well, some shepherds arrived and said that angels had told them about the birth of the baby.

19

Jacob   *(his eyes opening wide in amazement)* Angels?

Shem   Yes. They said that this baby was to be a king.

Jacob   A king! That baby! But they were only peasants!

Shem   They said you had told them that your inn was full.

Jacob   *(shaking his head)*   I don't believe it. They came but I sent them away. I was expecting someone quite different. Fancy you having a king under your roof! It was fortunate you had a room for them.

Shem   *(surprised)*   But I didn't have a room. I told you — all my rooms were full. They had to sleep in the stable. It was the only place I could find.

Jacob   And I had an empty room here all the time. If only I had known . . .

SHEM and JACOB quietly part, each entering his own inn.

Curtain

A LITTLE HOUSE

by

Jennie Austerberry

A LITTLE HOUSE

CAST

RHODA, a girl of Bethlehem
RACHEL, the innkeeper's daughter
HANNAH, Rhoda's mother
ABIGAIL, Rachel's mother
MARY
JOSEPH
Three WISE MEN (one African or Indian)

SCENES

1   The roof-top of Rhoda's house, and the street below. Christmas eve.
2   The stable of the inn, and the street. Christmas morning.
3   As Scene 1. The evening of Epiphany.
4   Inside Rhoda's house. Later the same night.

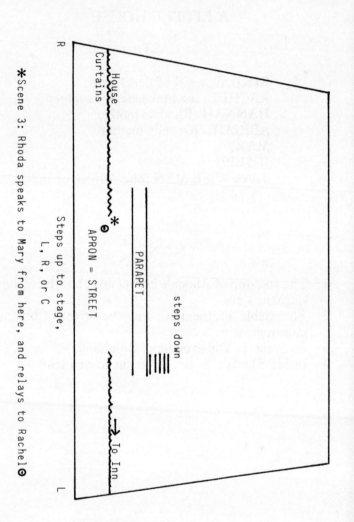

Steps up to stage,
L, R, or C

APRON = STREET

PARAPET

steps down

House
Curtains

To Inn

*Scene 3: Rhoda speaks to Mary from here, and relays to Rachel☉

24

PRODUCTION NOTES

Assuming full stage facilities with an apron stage　　　For
scenes 1 and 3, the curtains can be partly opened, and
across the gap some item placed to represent the parapet
of the roof (eg, a tall bookcase, back to audience, covered
with painted cardboard or hessian). This must be
sufficiently solid for the children to lean on. They can
then stand behind it on a plank between two chairs, with
space to allow them to descend. This will give them extra
height above the 'street'. (See diagram.)

Assuming performance in a church　　　Imagination must
be used. The pulpit could become the house roof; an area
curtained off for the stable; and a screened area for the
house interior.

Stage directions are given assuming presentation of the
play on a full stage; for presentation in a church, adapt as
necessary.

Carols may be sung off-stage between the scenes. The
following are suggested:
Between Scenes 1 and 2: O little town of Bethlehem; verses
1 and 2, sung softly.
Between Scenes 2 and 3: Once in royal David's city; verses
1 and 2, sung softly.
Between Scenes 3 and 4: We three kings of orient are;
verses 1, 2 and 3, sung softly.
After the final curtain: We three kings of orient are; verse
4, softly and slowly; verse 5, loudly and triumphantly.

SCENE 1

RHODA and RACHEL are standing on the roof-top of Rhoda's house, leaning over the parapet.

Rhoda   What an exciting day! I shouldn't think there have ever been such crowds in Bethlehem before.

Rachel   You should see our inn! Camels and horses and donkeys jostling each other in the yard, masters shouting to their servants, servants shouting to each other — you never heard such a noise! I was glad to get away from it and come up here for a bit!

Rhoda   I've been up here most of the day. I've had a grand view of all the people arriving. Is the inn full?

Rachel   I should just think it is! More than full! Daddy says the very walls will be bulging soon, if any more people come.

Rhoda   I don't suppose they will now. It's almost dark.

Rachel   Did you see the two Roman soldiers?

Rhoda   No, what are *they* doing here?

Rachel   Daddy says they'll be going to every house in the village, putting down the names of all the people.

Rhoda   Whatever for?

Rachel   It's for the Emperor. He wants to know just how many people there are in the country. Something to do with taxes, I think, but I don't really understand. That's what all the people are here for; didn't you know? You have your name put down in the place from which your family came, Daddy told me. I say, I'll have to go now. It must be nearly bedtime.

Rhoda   Mine too! There's nothing more to see, anyway. There isn't a person in sight.

Rachel   Yes, there is. A man and woman. Right down the street there.

> *She points towards back of audience. MARY and JOSEPH come slowly from back of hall, JOSEPH with his arm round MARY, looking anxiously at her from time to time.*

Rhoda   How tired she looks, and how slowly they are walking. They must have come a long way.

> *MARY and JOSEPH climb steps onto stage, walk across, and exit Stage L.*

Rachel   They're going towards our inn, but I shouldn't think they'll get a bed there! I wonder what they will do?

Rhoda   Perhaps your father will find some place for them to sleep. I do hope so.

Rachel	I'll run home and see. Tell you in the morning. Goodnight.
	Exits Stage L.
Rhoda	I'm coming down, too. Goodnight.
	Exits Stage R, into house interior.

SCENE 2

The stage curtains are closed on the stable scene. Rachel enters in front of curtains Stage L, and runs across the stage, calling as she runs.

Rachel	Rhoda! Rhoda!
	RHODA comes to meet her, in front of curtains Stage R.
Rhoda	Hello, you *are* early! I've only just got up!
Rachel	Oh, Rhoda, what do you think? There's a baby in our stable!
Rhoda	A baby? In the stable? What do you mean?
Rachel	You know those two people we saw last night, just before I went home? There wasn't any room for them in the inn, but Daddy let them have a corner of the stable to sleep in. And this morning there was a *baby*

there with them, the sweetest baby you ever saw. Oh, Rhoda, do come and see!

HANNAH enters in front of curtains Stage R.

Hannah   What's that you say? A baby born in the stable? Oh, the poor mother! I must go at once and see what I can do for her.

Rachel   *(as they cross towards Stage L)* I expect Mother is there by now. When I came out she was warming some water to wash the baby.

They exit Stage L. As they do so, the stage curtains open to reveal stable scene. MARY is seated on straw with baby on her knee. Her cloak has fallen off one shoulder, and JOSEPH is bending to replace it. As he does so, he looks over her shoulder at the baby, smiling, and gently touches his cheek with the knuckle of one finger. ABIGAIL is standing with a bowl of water and towel, to left of Mary. As she puts the bowl down on the straw, HANNAH'S voice is heard off left.

Hannah   *(off)*   Is this where they are, Rachel?

Rachel   *(off)*   Yes, this is the place.

HANNAH enters, followed by RHODA and RACHEL.

Abigail   *(turning and looking at Hannah)*   Why,

29

Hannah, what brings you here at this early hour?

Hannah   Rachel has just told me about the baby, and I came to see if I could help. *(Catching sight of the baby as she comes forward)* Oh, the sweet little moppet!

RHODA and RACHEL run to MARY, and sit one on each side of her, admiring the baby.

Abigail   It is good of you, Hannah. I am trying to do what I can, too. I could hardly sleep last night for thinking of this poor woman being out here, but what could we do? The inn was nearly bursting as it was, and it was either that or turning them away — and she was in no fit state to journey further.

Mary   You have been so kind to us. You brought us food, and gave us clean straw to lie on, and a blanket to keep us warm — and now you have brought water to wash our baby.

Joseph   We will never forget your goodness to us.

Hannah   But, Abigail, why didn't you send them to *me*? We would gladly have taken them in.

Abigail   I thought you would perhaps have other guests, and besides . . .

Hannah   You can't let them stay *here*. They must come home with me. We'll be glad to have them.

Rhoda   Oh, how lovely!

Joseph   If we *could* find somewhere to stay until my
              wife is strong enough to make the long
              journey to our home again . . . I'm a
              carpenter, and I could earn enough to keep
              us. We wouldn't want to be a burden.

Hannah   Then that's settled. You may come to us,
              and welcome. I'll hurry back now to prepare
              a meal for you, and a bed for the baby.
              Rhoda, wait here and bring our guests home
              when they're ready.

Rhoda   *(jumping up)*   Yes, Mother, I will.

              Exit HANNAH Stage R.

              Oh, please, may we help to wash the baby?

              *She takes the towel from ABIGAIL as
              the curtain falls.*

SCENE 3

*A few days later. As Scene 1, but the lights are dimmer: a
moonlight effect. RHODA and RACHEL are leaning on the
parapet.*

Rhoda   How lovely the stars are tonight. Look at
              that great big one up there. *(Pointing)* I
              never saw such a bright one before.

Rachel   *(looking up)*   Where? Oh, I see. Isn't it
              brilliant?

They both gaze at the stars for a moment.

How much longer will Mary and Joseph be staying with you?

Rhoda I don't know. A long time, I hope. I wish they could stay for ever, and never go back to Nazareth. Joseph has plenty of work to do here. He is always busy.

Rachel People say he's a good carpenter.

Rhoda And Mother loves having Mary with us. They talk together like old friends. And as for little Jesus . . .

Rachel He *is* sweet, isn't he?

Rhoda He's the most wonderful baby that ever was, since the world began — that's what I think! Mary lets me nurse him sometimes, and he looks at me with his big eyes — I'm sure he knows me and loves me already.

Rachel Do you think Mary would let *me* . . .

Rhoda Look! Who are those men down there? *(Pointing to back of audience)* They're coming this way.

Three WISE MEN come from back, through audience.

Rachel *(in a whisper)* What gorgeous robes! They must be very important people.

Rhoda   They look like foreigners to me. Yes, look, one of them's black! Whatever can they be doing in Bethlehem?

> *The three men arrive on the stage, and look up at the children. RHODA leans over to look at them.*

Wise Man 1   *(calling)*   Come down, child, if you please. We need your help.

> *RHODA draws back a little, and looks nervously at Rachel.*

Wise Man 2   *(imperiously)*   What's the matter, child? Why do you keep us waiting? We have come a long journey and wish to reach our goal.

Rhoda   *(in a whisper to Rachel)*   I'm frightened. What shall I do?

> *WISE MAN 2 begins to look angry, but WISE MAN 3 (an African or Indian) comes forward and lays a restraining hand on his arm.*

Wise Man 3   *(gently, looking up at the children)*   Have no fear. No one will harm you. We only wish to speak with you.

Rhoda   *(smiling)*   We're coming.

> *They disappear from roof.*

Wise Man 2   Why should they be afraid of us?

Wise Man 3   You forget how strange we must seem to them. Here they come — be gentle with them!

> *RHODA and RACHEL appear from house steps and walk shyly to front of stage.*

Rhoda   How can we help you, sirs? Are you looking for someone?

Wise Man 1   Tell us, please, where is the baby, the new-born king?

Rhoda   *(laughing)*   Do you mean our little Jesus? He's the only baby in this street, but he isn't a king, sirs. His mother and father are just ordinary people who came to Bethlehem for the census. They had nowhere to stay but the inn stable, so my mother let them stay with us. Oh, no, Jesus is the most wonderful baby in the world, but he isn't a king!

> *The WISE MEN look at one another and talk together, backs to the children.*

Wise Man 1   Jesus! Saviour! It must be he! Didn't I say that the star was shining directly above this house?

Rachel   *(gazing upwards, wonderingly)*   The star!

Wise Man 2   But so *small* a house? And ordinary working people? How can it be?

Wise Man 3 *(eagerly)* Take us to him, please.

Rhoda   This way, sirs.

> *She goes to curtain Stage R and speaks to someone within the house (see stage diagram for positioning).*

Mary, here are some visitors come to see Jesus. I can't think why they . . .

> *The WISE MEN brush her aside and go in. Rhoda looks inside, and calls in a hushed voice to Rachel, who is standing close behind her.*

Rachel, they are *kneeling* in front of Jesus! Now one is taking something from inside his robes . . . Rachel, I think it is *gold*! He is putting it down . . . it must be a present! Now the second one is giving him a present, too! Oh, what a lovely smell! It must be perfume. I can't see what the third one is giving him but . . . why, Rachel, for a moment Mary looked frightened, and held Jesus very close! Oh, it's all right — she's smiling now, and thanking them. They're standing up again. I think they're leaving. Let's go up on the roof again, and we can watch them going away.

> *They run round to roof steps and climb to the parapet. The WISE MEN re-enter from behind curtain Stage R.*

Wise Man 1 We will seek shelter in the inn tonight, but

35

tomorrow we must make our way back to Jerusalem.

Wise Man 2 Yes, we must keep our promise to King Herod, and tell him where the baby king is to be found.

Wise Man 3 No doubt he, too, will hasten to kneel before him, as we have done.

They cross stage, and exeunt left.

Rachel They're going to the inn. Won't Daddy be surprised!

Rhoda Rachel, did you hear what they said? That King Herod will come *here* to see Jesus. Do you think he really will come to our little house?

Rachel Perhaps he will! But, Rhoda, why did they still call Jesus a king? They must have seen that he was only a poor baby.

Rhoda And why did they give him those wonderful presents? I'm going in to look at them!

Rachel And I'm going home to see what's happening there! *(She is turning to leave when she has a sudden thought, and looks upwards, pointing.)* Look, Rhoda, the star *is* right over this house, just as they said.

Both stand looking up at the star as the curtain falls.

SCENE 4

Later that night. RHODA is asleep on a mat bed, down left; MARY and JOSEPH on mats down right; the baby in a cradle beside them. There is a wooden chest centre back, beside which stand the Wise Men's gifts. A knapsack hangs on a nail near them, and a length of rope is thrown carelessly in one corner. The light is dim, but a shaft of moonlight shines down on Mary and Joseph.

Joseph   *(in his sleep)* Lord, we will go at once. Nothing shall harm him while I am here to protect him.

He sits up, and looks round for a moment, bewildered. Then he rises and bends over MARY, shaking her shoulder. As he speaks, RHODA starts up, listening.

Mary! Mary! Wake up! Our baby is in danger!

Mary   *(leaning on her elbow, and speaking with bewilderment and mounting fear)* What is it, Joseph? Jesus in danger? What do you mean?

Joseph   Don't be frightened, dear Mary. God has spoken to me in a dream; we must go at once with our baby to Egypt, for King Herod will try to kill him.

Rhoda   *(jumping up and running to Joseph, clutching at his arm)* It isn't true! It can't be true! Who could want to harm such a beautiful baby? *(She begins to sob)*

37

Joseph   *(gently, with a hand on her shoulder)*   God does not lie, child. I do not understand, but I know it is true.

> *MARY has risen, and picked up the baby, holding him close.*

Rhoda   *(brushing away her tears and speaking firmly)*   Then you must go — at once! Shall I wake Mother? She will help you collect your things together.

Mary   No, don't wake her. She needs her sleep after a hard day's work. Will you help us instead?

Rhoda   Willingly! First I'll fetch a lantern, then I'll find food for your journey.

> *She goes out, R. MARY lays the baby on her mat, then goes to chest, taking from it clothes, etc, which she makes into a bundle. RHODA returns with lantern, which she places on the chest. The stage lightens as she comes in. She goes out again.*

Joseph   We must not forget the gifts brought to our baby this evening.

> *He takes down the knapsack and puts the gifts into it, putting it on his back. RHODA returns with a bundle of food.*

Rhoda   *(giving the food to MARY)*   Here are figs and bread. It is all I could find. And Joseph, will you take one of our sleeping-mats for Mary to lie on when you stop to rest? I know Mother will not mind.

Joseph How thoughtful you are, child. Yes, I will take one, for we may have strange resting places before our journey is over. And now, goodbye, Rhoda, and thank you. You have done all you could for us. Now you must try to sleep again, and in the morning tell your parents how it was that we had to leave so hurriedly. I'm sure they will understand.

Mary And tell them, too, that we thank them with all our heart for the kindness which they have shown to us and our baby. Goodbye, little one. *(She kisses RHODA)*

> *While Joseph and Mary have been speaking, RHODA has rolled up a mat and tied it with the rope. She now gives it to JOSEPH who puts it across his shoulders, holding the ends of rope over one shoulder.*

Joseph Do not fear for us, child. We are in God's hands, and no harm can come to us. Jesus is safe in his care. Come, Mary. *(Looking off L)* See how brightly the moon shines to light us on our way.

> *They are about to go when RHODA speaks tearfully.*

Rhoda May I give Jesus one last kiss before you go? I may never see him again.

39

*She does so. Then MARY goes out L,
followed by JOSEPH, the mat still slung
across his shoulders. RHODA stands
looking after them.*

They are almost at the corner. Soon I shall
lose sight of them. They've gone! No, they
were in the shadows — now they are in the
moonlight again — Joseph's arm is around
Mary — they look almost like one figure.
Oh, goodbye, little Jesus. God keep you
safe. How strange their shadow looks, with
the mat slung across Joseph's shoulders —
why, it is just like a great, dark cross!

Curtain

'LET ME IN!'

by

Jennie Austerberry

'LET ME IN!'

CAST

MARY
JOSEPH
INNKEEPER
INNKEEPER'S WIFE
NICODEMUS, a rich nobleman
RACHEL, his wife
Two SHEPHERDS
SHEPHERD BOY

Servants
Voices of guests and servants at inn
Voice of Christ-child
Voices of sleepers

The action takes place at the first Christmas, in the courtyard and guest room of the inn at Bethlehem.

SCENE 1

The courtyard of the inn. The curtains remain closed during the first exchanges, which should be shouted from one side of the stage to the other, to the accompaniment of sounds of running feet.

Various Voices

> Here, take my horse. Look lively!
> Coming, sir, fast as I can!
> Show this gentleman to his room!
> This way, sir!
> Where's that wine I ordered?
> How much longer have we to wait for a meal?

> *The curtains open. Servants are running to and fro with wine, food, blankets, etc. JOSEPH stands centre stage, with his arm round MARY. They are looking round, bewildered by the bustle. No one takes any notice of them. There is a lull, and MARY speaks. During the following conversation an occasional servant passes behind the speakers.*

Mary There will be no room here, Joseph. We shall have to go on.

Joseph We can but try. Maybe there is *somewhere*. I must find shelter for you soon, my dearest. You know that. *(He calls off right)* Innkeeper! Are you there?

> *Enter INNKEEPER, looking harassed.*

Innkeeper	*(brusquely)* What is it? What do you want?
Joseph	We are seeking a room for the night, and I wondered . . .
Innkeeper	*(laughing loudly)* You might as well ask for the moon! You'll find no room in Bethlehem tonight! I suppose you've come for the census, like all the rest?
Joseph	Yes, indeed. I am of the family of David, and so needs must . . . but we are late in arriving, I know. You see, my wife could not hurry. She . . .
	The INNKEEPER'S WIFE has appeared behind him, and whispers in his ear. He looks quickly at MARY, suddenly serious.
Innkeeper	I would help you if I could, but what can I do? You see what it is like!
Wife	*(to her husband)* There's the cave.
Joseph	*(with sudden hope)* The cave?
Innkeeper	It's in the hillside at the back there. We keep our own animals in it. But it's hardly fit . . .
Wife	We could put down clean straw, and I can find a blanket or two. It will give you shelter, if not much comfort.
Mary	Don't worry, Joseph. We shall be warm and dry there. *(To the wife)* Thank you for your kindness. Will you show us the way?

45

Innkeeper   Wait! I have just thought . . . there *is* one room still not occupied. It was ordered many days ago for my lord Nicodemus. He is a frequent visitor here, and I dare not offend him. But it *is* getting late. Maybe he will not come tonight. In that case . . .

Nicodemus   *(off left, loudly and imperiously)*   Make way there! Out of our way, if you please! We are expected!

Wife   That's Nicodemus now.

> *Enter NICODEMUS left, followed by RACHEL. The INNKEEPER hurries across stage, bowing as NICODEMUS enters.*

Nicodemus   *(speaking as he enters)*   Ho, there, innkeeper! Take us to our room at once! We've had a long journey, and we're cold and tired.

Innkeeper   Certainly, sir! At once, sir!

> *As he turns to lead the way, his eyes meet MARY's, and he stops dead, hesitates, then turns back to Nicodemus.*

There is just one thing, sir. This poor woman has just arrived with her husband, and I can offer them nothing better for the night than the cave where we house our animals. As you see, sir, she is in no fit state for such privation, and I thought . . . that is . . . well, it occurred to me that perhaps . . . that you might be willing . . . of your generosity . . . *(in a rush)* to sleep there yourself with the husband — I would make you as comfortable as possible — and allow her to occupy your bed in your wife's room. *(NICODEMUS is showing outraged indignation. The INNKEEPER stops nervously, then goes on boldly.)* She may well need the help of another woman before morning, sir.

Nicodemus How dare you! I have never been so insulted! Would you put *me* in a stable, and give this woman *my* . . .

> *As he says 'this woman' he turns with a gesture towards MARY, and his voice dies away. He stares for a moment, then speaks in a different voice.*

And yet . . . one must not be too hard . . . under the circumstances. Rachel, my dear, do you think . . .?

Rachel *(drawing herself up, indignantly)* What are you saying? Can you possibly be suggesting that *I* should act as midwife to some poor country-woman? What is she to me? And as for your sleeping in a cave — your place is by my side, I would have you know, and there you will be tonight. Innkeeper, show us to our room.

> *The INNKEEPER turns and leads off right, followed by RACHEL. NICODEMUS shrugs and follows.*

Wife   Come, my dear, I will show you the cave. It won't be so bad. The animals keep it warm, and you can at least rest.

> *She puts her arm round MARY, and leads her off left, followed by JOSEPH.*

SCENE 2

A guest room in the inn. NICODEMUS and RACHEL are lying on sleeping-mats, covered by blankets. Nicodemus is sound asleep, Rachel tossing restlessly and muttering.

Rachel   *(in her sleep)*   What is she to me? What is she to me?

> *Distant knocking.*

Voice of child
> *(off, as if at some distance)*   Let me in! Let me in!

Voices   *(off left)*   No room! No room!

> *Distant knocking.*

Voice of child
> *(distant)*   Let me in! Let me in!

Voices   *(off right)*   No room! No room!

> *Distant knocking.*

Voice of child
> *(distant)*   Let me in! Let me in!

Voices   *(off left and right)* No room! No room! No room!

> *Knocking at door R.*

Voice of child
> *(loud, and immediately behind door R.)* Let me in! Please let me in!

Rachel   *(in sleep)* No! No! No! There is no room here!

> *She starts up and gazes around, bewildered. The child's footsteps are heard running away in the distance. RACHEL rises from bed.*

What have I done?

> *She runs to door right, calling.*

Come back! Come back!

> *She returns to centre stage, sobbing, face in hands. NICODEMUS sits up.*

Nicodemus What's to do, Rachel? Why are you out of bed?

Rachel   I had a dream — it *must* have been a dream, but it was so vivid. I heard a child, knocking at the doors of the inn, and calling 'Let me in!' And from behind every door came the answer, 'No room!' Then the child knocked at this door, and again he called, 'Let me in!' and I sent him away. Nicodemus, I sent him away!

49

Nicodemus Come, Rachel, it was but a dream! The loss of our child is preying on your mind still. It gives you such fancies.

Rachel We had him such a short time — only two days. And when he died, my heart died with him. It became a block of ice in my breast, and will never be melted.

Nicodemus You must not talk like that. Time will heal . . .

Rachel Listen! Did you hear something? Was that a baby's cry?

Nicodemus A baby? What baby? You're imagining things again.

Rachel No, no! That woman in the cave. You know that she . . .

Nicodemus The cave? It's much too far away to hear anything from there. Besides, as you said yourself, what is she to you? True, I felt a moment's pity for her, but you were right, of course. Lie down again now, and let us sleep. I'm tired.

> *He lies down, pulls blanket up to his head, and sleeps.*

Rachel I know what I said, and I meant it — then. But now, I hardly understand myself, but — oh, Nicodemus, when our baby was born, I had every care, every attention, and yet he died. And this poor woman — in a stable, with no one to — it's no good, Nicodemus, I must go to her.

There is no answer, and she goes across and leans over NICODEMUS.

Asleep already? Better so, perhaps. I must go very quietly.

She picks up a shawl from beside her mat, and winds it round her head. Exit right.

SCENE 3

The inn courtyard, later that night. The stage is dimly lit, and empty.

Nicodemus *(off right, calling)*   Rachel! Rachel!

He enters right.

Rachel! Where are you?

RACHEL, bareheaded, hurries in left.

Rachel   Here I am, Nicodemus.

Nicodemus Rachel, what *are* you doing out in this cold courtyard? In the middle of the night! And bareheaded, too! Where's your shawl?

Rachel   I wrapped it round the baby. Straw is so scratchy and . . .

Nicodemus Baby? Straw? Rachel, what *are* you talking about? Wait a minute! I'm beginning to understand. Do you mean to tell me that you actually went to . . .

Rachel To the cave! Yes! I wondered if I should find it at first, but there was a lantern on a ledge inside, and its light showed me the entrance. And when I looked in, the baby had been born! The mother was lying back on the straw, tired out, and the husband was trying to wrap the bands round the child. He was doing his best but, oh dear, did you ever know a man who knew the least thing about looking after babies? Such a mess he was getting into! *(She laughs merrily)* So I asked him to let me help, and he was only too glad to . . .

Nicodemus Rachel, you laughed! I haven't heard you laugh since . . .

Rachel *(suddenly sober)* I know! I thought I should never laugh again! But tonight, I can't explain it, but you see — when I had wrapped the bands round the baby, I picked him up, and held him for a moment close to me. And in that moment, suddenly my heart felt warm again, as if the ice had melted, and I felt a great happiness!

> *She stands silent for a moment, serious and thoughtful, then, joyful again, turns to her husband.*

Then the mother said, 'Will you lay him in

the manger? Joseph has put clean straw there.' Wasn't that a good idea? It made a perfect little crib for him, only, as I said, straw is so scratchy, so I took off my shawl, and . . .

She stops as voices are heard off L.

Shepherd 1 This is the most likely place.

Enter TWO SHEPHERDS and BOY.

Shepherd 2 What makes you think so?

Shepherd 1 Well, there's no baby due in the village, that I do know. So they must be travellers. And if so, they may well be at the inn.

Shepherd 1 But the angel spoke of a manger. I remember his exact words: 'You will find a baby wrapped in strips of cloth and lying in a manger.' That sounds like a stable.

Boy I know where there's a stable. At least, it's a cave really, but the innkeeper uses it as a stable, so I suppose there'll be a manger in it. It's in the hillside at the back of the inn. I'll take you there.

Shepherd 1 But, is it possible? 'A Saviour, Christ the Lord' — that's what the angel called him. In a *manger*?

Shepherd 2 And then that glorious heavenly choir that we heard. 'Glory to God in the highest' they sang. And all for a baby born in a *stable*?

Boy   Oh, come *on*! The angel said a manger, and I know where a manger is. So why are we waiting?

> *He catches at the cloak of one shepherd, and drags him out. The other shepherd follows.*

Nicodemus Now what was all that about? The world's going mad, it seems! Come to bed, Rachel! *(He moves towards exit R. turning to speak as he reaches it)* Angels! Heavenly choirs! What next?

> *Exit NICODEMUS R. RACHEL hesitates, looking back to where shepherds have gone.*

Rachel   *(softly)* What next indeed!

> *She turns and follows her husband off R.*

> *Curtain*

NO ROOM

by

Noelene Martin

NO ROOM

CAST

MOTHER
RACHEL
MARTHA
INNKEEPER
MARY
JOSEPH
Four SHEPHERDS

Carol singers (off stage)
A voice (off stage)

During the play, Rachel changes from modern dress to traditional dress, and back again. Mother is in modern dress; Martha in traditional dress. A similar item of clothing, eg a scarf, can be worn by both women to suggest a link between the characters. The shepherds, innkeeper, Mary and Joseph wear traditional dress.

A couch is placed at one side of the stage and remains there for the whole play. It is completely ignored by the biblical characters.

SCENE 1

Mother (*hurrying in*) Rush, rush, rush. Every Christmas it's the same story. It's high time I sat down and rested my weary bones for a few minutes. (*She sits on the couch, sighs and relaxes*)

Rachel (*entering*) Hey, Mum. Is my costume ready for the school play tomorrow?

Mother Yes, dear. It only needs a quick iron and it's finished.

Rachel That's a relief.

Mother Do you know all your lines?

Rachel (*confidently*) Yes. (*She hesitates*) Well, I think so.

Mother (*sighing*) Where's the paper? I'll go over them with you.

Rachel (*complaining*) I was just going to get an apple. I'm starving!

Mother You can have an apple when I've heard you say your part.

Rachel (*resignedly*) Oh, all right. (*She gives MOTHER a crumpled piece of paper*) There isn't much to say. I'm the narrator. (*She points to the place*) See, at the top of the page.

Mother	Right. Go on. *(Prompting)* 'The Emperor Augustus . . .'
Rachel	'The Emperor Augustus had ordered a census and everyone had to return to their own town.' Um . . .
Mother	'Joseph took Mary . . .'
Rachel	Yes, I know. *(Speaking with little expression)* 'Joseph took Mary his wife to Bethlehem and the time came for her to have her baby. She wrapped her first son in strips of cloth and laid him in a manger because there was no room for them in the inn.' How's that?
Mother	It still needs some practice. *(She puts the paper down on the couch)* You know, that's always worried me.
Rachel	What, learning a part in a play?
Mother	No. That there was no room for Mary and Joseph in the inn.
Rachel	But, Mum, everyone knows that there were crowds of people in Bethlehem. They probably weren't the only ones not to find a place.
Mother	*(concerned)* But someone must have realised that they were special.
Rachel	*(shaking her head)* No, Mum. Mary and Joseph were just ordinary people and no one took any notice of them. They were too busy

59

with their own matters. *(Brightening)* Can I have an apple now?

Mother *(absentmindedly)* Yes, go on.

RACHEL exits.

There must have been some way of recognising them. I'm sure if I'd been there I would have noticed, and the story would have been quite different. *(She lies back on the couch and closes her eyes, muttering to herself)* I would have known . . . I would have known . . . I would . . .

Music is played to indicate a change of time and scene.

Innkeeper *(entering, calling)* Martha! Martha! Where is she?

He turns to RACHEL, now in biblical costume, who has followed him.

Rachel, do you know where your mother is?

Rachel The last time I saw her she was in the kitchen.

MARTHA enters carrying a broom.

Innkeeper Ah, there you are.

Martha Oh, I can't remember this inn being so busy. Why the Romans want to hold a census, I can't imagine.

Innkeeper   Taxes, my dear, taxes.

Martha   I don't think I can take any more running after guests. My poor feet. *(She rubs them)*

Innkeeper   You won't have to. We can lock the door now because the inn is full. *(He locks the door)*

Rachel   What happens if someone else knocks at the door, Dad?

Innkeeper   We just tell them to *(there is a knock at the door. He raises his voice)* GO AWAY! We're full!

Martha   *(doubtfully)* I suppose they'll find somewhere else to stay the night.

Rachel   *(confidently)* There must be plenty of rooms in Bethlehem. They won't have any trouble.

Innkeeper   And it's not our problem. We still have work to do here.

Martha   That's true, dear. Rachel, could you sweep the floor, please?

> *She gives RACHEL the broom and exits with the INNKEEPER. RACHEL begins to sweep the floor. A knock is heard at the door.*

Rachel   *(calling in direction of the door)*   We're full. I'm sorry.

The knocking persists and RACHEL goes to the door and opens it.

Joseph   Do you have a room for my wife and me for the night?

Rachel   I'm sorry, but the inn is full.

Innkeeper   *(entering and striding to the door)*   I thought I told you not to open the door, Rachel.

Rachel   *(turning to him)*   They kept knocking, Dad. I told them we have no room.

Innkeeper   *(turning to MARY and JOSEPH)*   You will have to go somewhere else.

Mary   There is no other place to go. We have tried everywhere.

Joseph   I wouldn't worry about myself, sir, but my wife is going to have a baby.

Rachel   A baby!

Joseph   Yes. So you see we are desperate for somewhere to stay.

Innkeeper   *(worried)*   Oh dear. Well the inn is full . . . the only place I can think of is our stable out the back.

MARTHA enters.

Rachel   The stable isn't a very nice place for a baby, Dad.

Mary	If it's all you have, we will take it and thank you for your kindness.
Martha	What's happening? What's all this about the stable?
Rachel	*(excitedly)* Mum, this lady is going to have a baby and they're going to stay in our stable tonight.
Martha	*(determinedly)* Oh, no, they're not!

Everyone looks at her in surprise.

Innkeeper	What do you mean, they're not? You can't just throw them out into the street.
Martha	I don't intend to do anything of the kind.
Innkeeper	*(confused)* Well, what *are* you going to do? Where are they going to stay?
Martha	In our room.
Innkeeper	*(incredulously)* What!
Martha	*(ignoring her husband's protest)* Rachel, take these people up to our room now. I'll be there in a minute to organise everything.
Joseph	*(protesting)* Thank you, but we really can't.
Mary	No. The stable will be fine.
Martha	*(firmly)* Indeed it won't. Come on, Rachel, show them the way.

MARY and JOSEPH follow RACHEL into the inn and off stage. The INNKEEPER turns to MARTHA in disbelief.

Innkeeper   Martha, what are you doing? Those people are total strangers — and you give them our room?

Martha   But she's going to have a baby, dear.

Innkeeper   That doesn't matter.

Martha   *(calmly)*   Yes, it does. They need our help and we must give them what we can. If anything happened to them, I would hate people to say that I didn't help because there was no room in our inn.

Exits in same direction as Mary and Joseph. RACHEL reappears and looks back over her shoulder at her mother.

Innkeeper   *(still dazed)*   What's got into your mother? She's turning the place upside-down.

They leave together, shaking their heads. Music is played to indicate a time lapse.

SCENE 2

The INNKEEPER is seated, writing. MARTHA rushes in.

Martha   *(excitedly)*   It's a boy, dear, it's a boy!

Innkeeper   *(annoyed at being interrupted)*   What's a boy? What are you talking about?

Martha   The baby. I've just seen him and they are going to call him Jesus.

Innkeeper   *(disinterestedly and looking back at his work)*   Jesus — how nice. *(Putting down his work and looking more cheerful)* Now perhaps we'll get some peace and quiet around here, though where we're going to sleep I don't know.

> *He looks around the room. There is a knock at the door.*

Oh, no, not again! *(Shouting)* Can't you read? The sign says 'Full'. Go away!

> *The knocking continues.*

They'll wake up the whole neighbourhood.

Martha   *(soothingly)*   I'll get it, dear. You never know who it might be.

Innkeeper   *(holding his head in his hands)*   Oh, no, not again!

MARTHA opens the door.

Shepherd 1 Excuse me. We know it's late, but we're looking for a baby born tonight. We were directed to your inn.

Martha How strange! Yes, we have a baby here. Come in and see him. *(Motions with her hand for them to enter)*

Shepherd 2 *(surprised)* Come in? In here?

Martha *(also surprised)* Why, yes. They are comfortable upstairs in our bedroom.

Shepherd 3 *(shaking his head)* Oh, no, I'm sorry. We've come to the wrong place.

Shepherd 4 You see, the baby we want was born in a stable.

The INNKEEPER stands and moves to the door.

Innkeeper In a stable? Who told you a thing like that? Who are you, anyway?

Shepherd 1 We're shepherds. We were watching over our sheep tonight when suddenly some angels came and told us about the birth of a baby.

Innkeeper Angels? I don't believe it.

Shepherd 2 It's true. They said we would find the baby in a manger and he is Christ the Lord.

Innkeeper   Christ the Lord? Now I *know* I don't believe it!

Shepherd 3 We're sorry to have bothered you.

Shepherd 4 Come on, we must keep looking.

The SHEPHERDS begin to leave.

Martha   No, wait. This is the right place.

Shepherd 1 But you said . . .

Martha   Yes, I know. But when they first arrived, my husband told them our inn was full. When he saw that she was going to have a baby, he offered them the stable, but then I . . .

Innkeeper   *(interrupting)* *We* decided that a stable was no place for a baby to be born, so we offered them our room.

Martha   And they are there now.

Shepherd 2 *(looking at the other shepherds)* Then this must be the place. Can we go and see the child?

Innkeeper   Come this way.

They all begin to walk across the stage.

Shepherd 3 It was kind of you to offer them help, especially as they must be strangers to you.

Martha   It was no trouble. I always try to help those in need. Never let it be said there was no

room in my inn . . . no room in my inn . . .
no room . . .

*They leave the stage with the last words
fading away. Music is played to indicate
the change of time.*

Mother   *(on the couch, beginning to stir,
mumbling)* No room in my inn . . . no
room . . .

*RACHEL enters, in modern dress, an
apple in her hand.*

Rachel   Did you say something, Mum? Were you
talking to me?

Mother   *(rubbing her eyes)*   Uh? Oh . . . I must have
dozed off. No, I don't think I said anything.
A sound of singing comes from off stage.

What's that singing?

Rachel   *(moving to window and looking out)*   There
are some carol singers out there, Mum. I'll
go and see.

*RACHEL exits. MOTHER shakes her
head vigorously.*

Mother   I must have been dreaming, yet it all seemed
so real.

*RACHEL re-enters as MOTHER sits
up on the couch.*

The carols sound nice.

Rachel   The singers are from the churches and they're collecting for the poor people in the Third World. Have you some money for them?

Mother   For the Third World? Money? Oh no, I really can't spare any. *(Shakes her head)*

Rachel   But Mum . . .

Mother   Look, Rachel, we've spent enough on Christmas already, what with cards and presents and food and everything. I'm not giving out any more. I haven't any money left for ourselves, let alone for people I know nothing about.

Rachel   *(resignedly)* OK, Mum.

> *She shrugs, picks up her papers from the couch and begins to walk across stage.*

Voice   *(off stage)* Jesus said, 'What you have done to the least of these my brothers and sisters you have done to me.'

Mother   What did you say, Rachel?

Rachel   *(surprised, turning to Mother)* Me? I was just reading my lines: 'She . . . laid him in a manger because there was no room for them to stay in the inn.'

> *RACHEL exits.*

Mother   *(repeating the words slowly)* No room in the

inn . . . no room in the inn . . .*(Suddenly jumping up from the couch, calling)* Rachel, call those singers back. I've changed my mind. I will give them some money!

She runs off stage.

THE WORST CHRISTMAS PLAY EVER

by

Noelene Martin

THE WORST
CHRISTMAS PLAY EVER

A play for six children and one adult

CAST

DAVID, playing the innkeeper
KAREN, playing Mary
CATHY, playing a shepherd
ANDY, playing a wise man
DANIEL, playing Joseph
LESLEY, playing an angel
MRS BATES

The children are dressed in 'traditional' costumes for a
Nativity Play. Mrs Bates is dressed in modern everyday
clothes.

The setting is a room behind the stage where the annual
Christmas play is to be performed. As the children enter,
they stand or sit on chairs, arranging their costumes and
props in preparation for the play which is about to
commence.

SCENE 1

Karen   *(calling over her shoulder as she enters)*   Come on. The play's going to start in a few minutes.

> *DAVID, DANIEL, LESLEY and CATHY enter.*

David   *(slumping into a chair)*   This is going to be the worst Christmas play ever.

Daniel   Don't be silly. It's not that bad.

Lesley   It's no different from the play we did last year.

Daniel   *(slightly bored)*   Or the year before that.

David   Yes it is. Take Terry for instance.

Lesley   Terry? *(Looking around)* Where is Terry?

David   That's what I mean. He's not here. He's sick.

Lesley   Oh no! Who's going to say his words?

Cathy   *(fixing her shepherd's headgear)*   Mrs Bates asked me to do it.

Karen   Well, what's the problem? No one in the audience will know we have one less shepherd.

Daniel *(giving Cathy a gentle nudge)* As long as Cathy remembers to say the lines.

Cathy *(smiling at him)* Don't worry — I'll remember.

David And speaking of lines, what about Andy? He hasn't said his part properly at any of the rehearsals.

Lesley Let's hope he gets it right tonight.

> *The others nod and murmur in agreement. ANDY enters.*

Daniel *(turning towards him)* Here's Andy. Hey, do you know your lines?

Andy *(offended)* Of course I know them. *(Proudly)* I've been practising all day. *(He stands in a pose as if to recite, waits for silence and then begins)*
'Gold is the gift I bring
For a child so young and small,
One day he'll be the king
. . . um . . . um . . .'
(He stops and looks around for help)

Everyone 'And Saviour of us all.'

Andy *(shaking his head)* I knew it a little while ago. *(He resumes his pose)*
'To save us one and all.'

Everyone No! *(They throw up their hands in exasperation)*

David	I told you. This is going to be the worst Christmas play ever.
Lesley	*(going up to Andy)* Why can't you remember your lines, Andy? I know my part. *(She too poses for her recitation)* 'Do not be afraid for I bring . . .'
Karen	*(interrupting her)* It's all right for you — you've got words to learn. *(Pointing to herself)* What about me? Here am I, Mary, a very important person in the play, and I don't say anything.
Daniel	Well, I'm Joseph, and he's important too, but I don't say much, either.
Karen	You ask if there is room for us at the inn. I just stand there and look stupid.
Cathy	You do that very well, Karen.
	Everyone laughs.
Andy	At least you don't have to talk to a doll like I do.
Daniel	But it won't be a doll tonight, Andy.
David	And that's another thing. Why can't we have a doll for the baby Jesus like everyone else does? Why do we have to have a *real* baby?
Karen	*(defensively)* I think it's a good idea.

David   That's because it's your sister.

Daniel   You can't have a girl playing the baby Jesus. *(The idea has obviously just struck him)*

Lesley   Why not?

Daniel   Because Jesus was a boy, of course.

Karen   Well, we haven't any baby boys available, and I don't think it makes any difference. Sophie will make a lovely baby Jesus.

Andy   *(shaking his head and looking worried)* I hope she doesn't cry all the time like *my* sister used to. No one will hear the play.

Karen   *(reassuringly)* I don't think she'll cry. She's usually very good.

Cathy   *(in a dreamy voice)* I think it's a pity Mrs Bates didn't let me bring a live sheep as well . . .

David   Live sheep . . . a live baby . . . *(throws his hands into the air)* . . . I tell you, this is going to be the worst Christmas play ever.

        MRS BATES bustles in with a worried expression on her face.

Mrs Bates   All right, everyone, we're about to start. Are you all ready?

Everyone   Yes, Mrs Bates.

Mrs Bates   Good. Now, Cathy, you'll remember to say Terry's lines, won't you?

Cathy   Yes, Mrs Bates.

Mrs Bates   Mrs Harrison has Sophie ready for the manger scene. *(She catches sight of Andy)* Andy, do you know your words?

Everyone except Andy
No!

Mrs Bates   *(shaking her head)*   Well, do your best. I'll prompt from behind the curtain.

> *The children collect their props, ready to leave.*

Mrs Bates   Lesley, your costume is crooked. Wait a minute. *(She adjusts the costume)*

David   *(standing up)*   Oh, goodness. I tell you . . .

Everyone except David and Mrs Bates
(in a chorus which mimics David's expression) This is going to be the worst Christmas play ever!

> *The CHILDREN and MRS BATES exit.*

SCENE 2

It is the same room and the play is over. The CHILDREN re-enter, taking off their headgear and putting down their props.

Daniel   *(relieved)*   I'm glad that's over.

Lesley   *(sighing)*   Me too. I always get nervous in front of a lot of people.

Karen   Andy didn't seem to be nervous. He even remembered all his lines.

Daniel   *(patting Andy on the back)*   Yes, good work, Andy. You didn't miss a word.

Andy   *(embarrassed)*   It didn't seem so silly giving a present to a baby. At the rehearsals, the doll just lay there, but Sophie even held her little hands up to me as if she really wanted the gift. The words just came easily.

Cathy   I was worried when Sophie began to cry.

Lesley   So was I, but she stopped almost immediately when Karen picked her up.

Cathy   And it looked so natural — the sort of thing Mary would have done with Jesus.

Daniel   I think it was only then that some people in the audience realised it was a real baby. It caused quite a stir.

Everyone nods their head in agreement.

Karen   Yes, all of a sudden everyone was looking at the *baby*, and I realised that that's how it should be. After all, the baby *is* the most important person in the Christmas story.

Andy   *(slowly and thoughtfully)* I think you're right, Karen. I hadn't thought of that before. I'd always thought that the character *I* played was the most important. I'd never really thought about the *baby* at all.

Lesley   I'm glad we had a real baby. What do you think, David?

> *Everyone turns to DAVID who has been sitting quietly since he entered.*

David   *(hesitating slightly)* I've been saying it all along. This was going to be the BEST Christmas play ever!

> *He turns and runs off quickly, with the rest following him.*

A NEW SONG

by

Noelene Martin

A NEW SONG

CAST

NARRATOR
JOSEPH MOHR
FRANZ GRUBER
WOMAN
KARL MAURACHER
MOTHER
FATHER
Four DAUGHTERS
MAN

Customers

The characters are dressed in warm clothing suitable for an Austrian winter in the early part of the 19th Century.

The acting area could consist of a church interior, with organ, at one side, a cottage interior at the other, with the space between as a footpath. The final scene takes place at the Leipzig Fair.

The Narrator remains seated at one side throughout. A spotlight can be used when the Narrator speaks.

SCENE 1

A church interior, lit by candles placed on and near the organ.

Narrator It is Christmas Eve in the year 1818. In Oberndorf, a village in the Austrian alps, the church organist, Franz Gruber, is working hard trying to mend the organ. The curate, Joseph Mohr, has come to check on the progress.

> *A clanking sound comes from behind the organ. JOSEPH enters.*

Joseph *(raising his voice)* How's it going, Franz?

> *The clanking stops. FRANZ emerges from behind the organ.*

Franz *(wiping his hands on a cloth)* I don't think I can fix it, Joseph. I have taken it to pieces and put it back together again, but it still won't go.

Joseph *(concerned)* But we need music for the midnight service.

Franz I know that, but there's nothing more I can do. I'm trying my hardest, but I'm an organist, not an organ mender.

Joseph There is still time. Keep working on it.

Franz *(hopefully)* Perhaps you can help me. If we both worked on it together . . .

Joseph   *(laughing)* I know even less about fixing organs that you do. No, I think the best plan is if I leave you alone. Besides, there are some families I would like to visit tonight.

Franz   *(holding up a piece of organ)* Joseph, you don't know where this goes, do you?

Joseph   *(shaking his head)* No idea. Do your best, Franz.

    JOSEPH leaves. FRANZ looks after him and throws his hands up in the air.

Franz   *(disgustedly)* Do my best! It's freezing in here, these candles keep flickering so that I can't see properly, and I don't know what I'm doing anyway. Do my best!

    He returns to his work, banging and clattering with his tools.

SCENE 2

Interior of a cottage. In one corner is a cot. A table and chairs are placed in the centre of the room. A fire is alight.

Narrator   While Franz struggled with the organ, the Revd Joseph Mohr spent the next couple of hours visiting parishioners.

JOSEPH knocks softly at the door and when there is no answer knocks again a little louder. A WOMAN rushes to the door, wiping her hands on a towel. She opens the door.

Woman Oh, it's you, Reverend Mohr. I didn't expect anyone to call tonight.

Joseph I won't come in if you're busy.

Woman Oh, no, come in. It's freezing out there. Come and warm yourself by the fire. You've given me an excuse to sit down for a while.

Joseph *(entering, rubbing his hands together to warm them)* I didn't want to knock too loudly in case I woke the children.

Woman I think they're all asleep now. They get so excited about Christmas it's hard for them to settle down. *(She points to the fire)* Please warm yourself, you must be frozen.

JOSEPH moves to the fire and warms his hands while the woman sits on a chair near the table.

Joseph It's certainly cold out, but it isn't snowing and the wind has dropped, so really it's quite pleasant walking at the moment. The night is clear, quiet and peaceful.

Woman I do so love a bright, clear night.

JOSEPH moves from the fire and sits on a chair. As he does so he suddenly remembers something and pulls a small parcel from his coat pocket.

Joseph   Oh, I nearly forgot. Maria asked me to give you this. It's a little present for the baby.

Woman   *(taking the parcel and putting it on the table)*   Thank you. How kind of her — and of you for bringing it.

Joseph   Not at all. Anyway it was a good excuse for me to see the baby. Is she asleep?

Woman   *(nodding)*   Sound asleep.

She points to the cot and JOSEPH tiptoes over and peeps in at the sleeping child.

Joseph   How sweet and innocent a new baby is.

Woman   Yes — and they bring such joy and happiness into a home, too.

JOSEPH returns to his chair.

Joseph   It's a very special time to have a baby — at Christmas, when we are celebrating the birth of our Lord.

Woman   I feel she's made the Christmas story very real for us this year.

JOSEPH nods and then stands, putting on his gloves and hat.

Joseph	I must go or you won't finish your preparations for tomorrow.
Woman	*(standing)* Thank you for coming and bringing the present, Reverend Mohr. I suppose the church will be full for the service tonight.
Joseph	I expect so, but we've been having some trouble with the organ. I've left Franz trying to fix it.
Woman	I didn't know Franz could mend organs!
Joseph	Neither did he, but I'm sure he'll manage somehow.

He opens the door.

Woman	*(looking out)* It does seem so quiet and peaceful out there, just as you said.
Joseph	Just like that baby of yours asleep in her cot. Goodnight.

JOSEPH exits. The WOMAN shivers and closes the door.

SCENE 3

JOSEPH is walking slowly back to the church. He looks all around, and up at the sky, and talks to himself.

Joseph   How still the night is . . . there isn't a sound anywhere . . . I wonder if it was on such a night as this that our Lord Jesus was born . . . a silent night . . . a holy night . . . the angels appeared to the shepherds . . . the star — brilliant in the sky, brighter than those shining now . . . on the night that Christ our Saviour was born . . .

Exits.

SCENE 4

The church interior. FRANZ is still hammering at the organ when JOSEPH rushes in.

Joseph   *(excitedly)* Franz! Franz! Listen to this! I've just . . . *(his excitement fades as FRANZ emerges, looking dusty and untidy)*

Franz   *(annoyed)* Just what?

Joseph   *(quietly)* Is it fixed yet?

Franz   *(still annoyed)* Fixed? No, Joseph, and it won't be fixed — not by me, anyway. I've spent hours on this thing and it still won't work.

Joseph   *(disappointedly)* But I've just written a poem and hoped you could put it to music and we'd sing it tonight at the service.

Franz   Well, we won't be singing to organ music tonight, that I can assure you.

Joseph   No music? What can we do?

Franz   *(off-handedly)*   I can always play my guitar.

Joseph   *(brightening)*   That will have to do. Do you think you can write a tune for my poem?

Franz   My time would be better spent doing that than fooling around here. You write out the words while I go home and have a wash and get my guitar.

Joseph   The congregation will be surprised — a new song for Christmas.

Franz   That won't be the only surprise!

Exeunt.

SCENE 5

In the church.

Narrator   So at that midnight service, 'Silent Night' was sung for the first time, accompanied by a guitar. Some time later, the organ builder, Karl Mauracher, arrived to mend the organ.

> *FRANZ and JOSEPH stand together talking quietly. KARL appears from behind the organ, wiping his hands. FRANZ and JOSEPH look at him hopefully.*

Karl   There. That should be all right now. I'm not surprised you had trouble, Franz. It was a difficult job.

Franz   I'm not an expert in that field, anyway.

Karl   Well, let us hear you do something you can do well. Play a tune and let me hear how the organ sounds.

> *FRANZ sits down and plays the tune of 'Silent Night'.*

Karl   *(nodding and smiling)* Oh, yes, that is perfect, perfect. *(He pats the organ lovingly)* This is indeed a fine instrument. But what tune did you play? I've never heard it before.

91

Franz   It is the tune I composed to accompany the words of a poem Joseph wrote on Christmas Eve.

Joseph   We sang it at the midnight service.

Karl   But what did you do for music if the organ wasn't working?

Franz   I played my guitar.

Karl   A guitar! How inventive. *(Turns to Joseph)* Have you the words of this poem?

Joseph   *(surprised)* Why, yes. I have them here with the music as well.

> *He gives KARL a sheet of paper. KARL hums a couple of lines.*

Karl   This is truly delightful. In the Zillertal valley where I live, there are four Strasser children who will love this. May I keep it?

Joseph   Yes, certainly. We have several more copies. I do hope they like it. We felt it was quite successful here.

> *KARL folds the paper and puts it in his pocket. Exeunt.*

SCENE 6

Street with stalls at Leipzig Fair, a few years later.

Narrator   The Strasser sisters did enjoy the song and sang it in concerts everywhere they went. One year they accompanied their parents to the Leipzig Fair where the family hoped to sell many pairs of hand-made gloves.

> *The Strasser family stands behind a stall covered with gloves. They hold them up, but no one passing takes any notice.*

Mother   Oh dear, we have our beautiful gloves here for sale but we can't seem to attract anyone's attention.

Father   *(shouting, holding up some gloves)* Come one, come all! Beautiful hand-made gloves for sale!

> *The people still walk straight past.*

Mother   *(shaking her head)* It's no use, dear. Everyone is shouting their wares. Your voice just mingles with the rest. We need something different. *(Pauses)* Perhaps the girls could sing.

Father   *(brightening)* That's a good idea. *(He motions to the girls)* Girls — stand near the stall and sing some of your favourite songs. It may attract the customers.

> *The girls come forward.*

Daughter 1   What shall we sing?

Mother   Something that will contrast with all the rush and bustle.

Daughter 2   *(turning to the others)* How about 'Silent Night'? No one here will have heard it, and Christmas is approaching.

Daughter 3   Good idea.

> *They all agree, and the GIRLS sing 'Silent Night'. CUSTOMERS, attracted by the girls' voices, pause and stop at the stall. They stand and listen, and some buy gloves. The GIRLS finish and the CUSTOMERS move away, except for one man.*

Man   *(to the parents)* May I congratulate you on your four beautiful daughters and their exquisite voices!

Father   *(flattered)* Thank you, sir.

Man   Perhaps I should introduce myself. I am the Director of Music for the Kingdom of Saxony. I am currently arranging an evening of music for the King and Queen on Christmas Eve. I would like your daughters to be a part of that evening and sing that delightful song.

> *The GIRLS and their PARENTS are very excited.*

Daughter 4   We're to sing before the King and Queen? We'll be famous!

Narrator   That Christmas Eve the girls sang 'Silent Night' before the King and Queen. Since then the song has travelled from country to country, gaining in recognition and popularity over the years. It is now one of the most popular Christmas carols and is sung at Christmas throughout the world — and all due to a broken organ.

> *The players and audience join in singing 'Silent Night' together.*